The Storm Has a Ministry Too

Wanda S. Briscoe

Foreword by J.E. Bamidele Sturdivant

THE STORM HAS A MINISTRY TOO
Copyright © 2019 by Wanda S. Briscoe

All rights reserved. This publication may not be reproduced, stored in a retrieval system, or transmitted in whole or in part, in any form or by any means, electronic, mechanical, photocopying, recording, or otherwise, without prior written permission of the publisher.

ISBN: 978-1-7339413-3-4

Unless otherwise indicated, all Scripture quotations are taken from the New King James Version (NKJV) of the Holy Bible. Copyright @ 1982 by Thomas Nelson, Inc. Used by permission.

Published in USA by Vision to Fruition Publishing House (www.vision-fruition.com)

Cover Design: LaKesha L. Williams

Vision to Fruition Publishing House is not responsible for any content or determination of work. All information is solely considered as the point of view of the author.

In loving memory of my youngest son, Darryl Bernard Dennis, II. Your life was tragically taken from us on December 3, 2018, while you were only 22 years old. There hasn't been a day that I haven't cried. I didn't ask God "why?", but instead I asked God, "What is it that He wants me to learn from this storm?" Keep smiling down on us with that beautiful smile of yours, and we will see each other again. Rest in Heaven my sweet baby boy!

Dedication

This book is an easy read and dedicated to everyone who is going through a storm and/or coming out of a storm. Sometimes the storms of life can get us off course with the extreme turbulence that they may bring, and we tend to lose focus on what is important. Let's walk together in **VICTORY**, as we embrace the freedom in whom God has called us to be!

Acknowledgments

It is impossible for me to acknowledge everyone who has impacted and poured wisdom into me. I am thankful for the people that have been planted in my life to help push, and birth out what God has placed in me. To my closest group of friends (you know who you are), who have encouraged me, prayed with and for me, let me vent, and counseled me; from the bottom of my heart, I Thank You!

- *My parents*: Bishop John W. Briscoe and First Lady Mary A. Briscoe, and my siblings, (Wesley, Wynne, Danielle, and Devon), my sister-in-love Linda, and my beautiful niece Cassandra, all of you are my biggest cheerleaders. I thank you for giving me the push that I needed, the encouragement, the correction, and all the pep talks. After many years of traveling back and forth from Atlanta to Maryland, I am so happy to be home with my family. May we treasure the new memories and moments in time that we are creating.

- *My sons*: Jarren, Jaquan, and Darryl II: God blessed me with three special gifts to love, to nourish, and to give back to Him. I thank each of you for never giving up on me when the going got rough. Early on, I made some mistakes trying to find my way as a young mother, but you showed me unconditional love in a world that is full of conditions. Keep God first in your lives, and always read and meditate on Psalms 91.

- *Faith United Ministries Family*: From my first visit to the church on November 6, 2016, I knew that this was the ministry I was to be planted in. Pastor J.E. Bamidele Sturdivant and Co-Pastor P.E. Sturdivant, are spiritual parents who are concerned about their sons and daughters in ministry, and I love their transparency and authenticity. My prayer is that God will continue to take our Pastor and Co-Pastor higher in Him as they lead us.

- *Dr. Janice Payne*: God truly placed you in my life. We laugh about our encounter, because we don't know how we met, or who introduced us, but since our divine connection in 2013, we have formed a bond that is unbreakable – similar to Naomi and Ruth. I thank you and your family for "adopting" me as one of your own. May God give you your hearts' desires, and I look forward to seeing your soul saving and deliverance plays turn into movies on the big screen!

- *Pink ~ Bold ~ and Beautiful*: This breast cancer "sisterhood" group of remarkable women is God ordained. We all have our different journeys with breast cancer, but our love and support for each other is unchanging. May each of you continue to sparkle and show the world that cancer does not define us – God does. For those in the group who have earned their angel wings, keep smiling upon us.

Table of Contents

Foreword 2
Preface 4
Chapter 1 The Crutch.. 7
Chapter 2 The Pain Had A Purpose 11
Chapter 3 The Tears of Hannah 17
Chapter 4 Words Have Power.................................... 21
Chapter 5 When God Interrupts Your Life 27
Chapter 6 Spiritual Health 33
Chapter 7 The Box... 37
Chapter 8 Is My "Yes" Negotiable? 39
Chapter 9 The Tsunami Called Grief......................... 41

A Collection of Poems Inspired by the Storm

Poem - I Am A Woman 47
Poem - Dear Butterfly.. 49
Poem - New Beginnings 50
Poem - God Had A Plan... 51
Poem - A House vs. A Home...................................... 52
Poem - The Darkest Moments Define My Life 53
Poem - My Journey.. 54
Poem - The Invisible Chain 55
30 Day Journal 59

Foreword

"The Storm Has a Ministry Too"

Adversity is an uncertain certainty. There is no doubt that it will come. It is unescapable. No amount of money, intelligence, or spirituality exempts one from the onslaught or the impact of trouble. It is part and parcel of the *human experience*. Job declared it this way, *"man who is born of a woman is of a few days and full of trouble."* – Job 14:1

The Lord, Jesus Christ, said it thusly –

"...in the world you will have tribulation, but be of good cheer, I have overcome the world."
John 16:33

So then, the challenge is: not to pretend that you are not going to encounter a storm, but to prepare for the conflict before it comes. *"How,"* you may ask, *"does one prepare for the unexpected?"* Simple....by focusing on strengthening *yourself*, and not giving your strength to the *storm*!

The late Dr. Myles Munroe stated – *"you will never be remembered by what you avoid, but by what you've survived."*
In this work, *"The Storm Has a Ministry Too,"* Wanda Briscoe takes us on a 'step by step' journey of emotions, encounters, and experiences that will force one to fortify their foundation, and reevaluate their faith, their family, their friends and their future. She

has *survived* and learned how to *thrive* on the "other side" of the storm.

I strongly recommend this work to you, and urge you to read it, meditate on its principles, and give copies of it to your friends.

God Bless you as you read.

J.E. Bamidele Sturdivant
Pastor
Faith United Ministries
District Heights, MD

Preface

"The storm that was sent to break you, is going to be the storm that God uses to make you"
~ **Author Unknown**

What is a storm? In the natural, a storm is a violent disturbance of the atmosphere with strong winds, usually rain, thunder, and lightening. As a child I was afraid of storms, and I would make my sister Wynne, get in the bed with me because I was terrified of the noise. I felt more comfortable having someone with me during a storm. In my life, I have been presented with multiple storms, and I reflect at how God took away my comfortability, and He has used my storms for His Glory. I read a profound quote that said, "Not all storms come to disrupt your life, some come to clear your path." That is a quote that we need to really ponder on, and look deep within, because maybe the storms that you are experiencing are a form of protection, and not to harm you.

Storms are also created when a center of low pressure develops with a system of high pressure surrounding it. For me, I found that my low-pressure points were self-esteem issues, resentment, bitterness, unforgiveness, abandonment issues, and being a people pleaser. The high pressure that was surrounding me was God trying to get me to draw closer to Him. God was trying to show me who I am, and whose I am. A storm can also be a sickness, a generational curse, a divorce, lack of finances, and emotional issues.

Julia Roberts is one of my favorite actresses, and in the movie Eat ~ Pray ~ Love, she was going through a divorce, and also going through the storm of finding herself as a woman. In the movie, the Italian word "Tutti" is mentioned, and it caught my attention. Some of the translations of the word "Tutti," are that it means "everybody," or my favorite translation is "When you set out in the world to help yourself, sometimes you end up helping Tutti." I found that word so powerful, and relatable, because I know that the storms that I have gone through were not solely about me. I believe that some of my storms were about me helping someone or everybody, so that God can get the glory, and I pray that you will be blessed by this book.

Chapter One

The Crutch

Definition of **crutch**: something that a person uses too much for help or support.

In 2014 and 2017, I had to have surgery on my left knee for osteoarthritis. Upon my discharge from the hospital, I was given a pair of crutches to walk with. The nurses adjusted the crutches to my height, and showed me how to walk with them, so that I wouldn't put a lot of pressure on my armpits. Even though I was shown by trained medical staff on how to properly use the crutches, they were still uncomfortable. For my first surgery, my mom made a "contraption" with a towel and wrapped it around the top of the crutch so that it wouldn't hurt underneath my arms. I used the crutches for several weeks, and then I realized that I was becoming dependent on them instead of trying to walk on my own.

One day I looked at the crutches, and it dawned on me how they symbolized some people that used to be in my life. I had used people as crutches. Even though they didn't necessarily "fit" me, I tried to adjust them to my life. I was forcing a square peg into a round hole. I wanted to fit in, and I didn't want to be alone in life. When we allow loneliness to be the driving force of entering relationships, it can have dire consequences. As long as I was dependent on people, I didn't need to walk on my own. I didn't need to walk in my calling that God had placed on my life, and I didn't need to depend on God. God has a way of turning things around and showing us that we are to depend on Him and not man, or things. In Proverbs 3:5, it states *"Trust in the Lord with all your heart and lean not unto your own understanding."* I had to do a self-check, and I realized that I wasn't trusting God with all my heart. I was trusting people without questioning their motives, which turned out to be detrimental in my life.

Things were totally different when I had my surgery in 2017 on the same knee. I tried walking with crutches, and I couldn't do it for one day. I wondered, what had transpired from 2014 to 2017, to the point where I wasn't depending on crutches? The surgery was on the same knee, so one would think that this wasn't new to me. But it actually was new, because in the course of three years, I had grown up spiritually. I didn't need the same people who were once my crutches. Previously, I was so dependent on people that I wouldn't speak up out of fear of having an opinion, or fear of confrontations. Now, I am walking more closely with God, and I am trusting God wholeheartedly, and all of this has made a huge difference in my life. If feels good to think on my own, to make sound decisions led by the Holy Spirit, and to have made God my crutch instead of man.

<u>Meditative Point</u>

Do your own self-check. Look deep within your soul and be honest with yourself to see if you have made people and/or things your crutch. If so, why haven't you totally trusted God? Do not let another day go by without releasing those people and/things. Pray and ask God to forgive you for not trusting Him completely and start TODAY trusting God.

Scripture Reference

Psalms 25:2
"Oh my God, I trust in You; let me not be ashamed; let not my enemies' triumph over me."

Chapter Two

The Pain Had A Purpose

Merriam Webster definition of "pain": usually localized physical suffering associated with bodily disorder (such as a disease or an injury); acute mental or emotional distress or suffering.

I will never forget the day that I received the telephone call that changed my life forever. It was January 19, 2011, and I can still hear my doctor's voice as if it was yesterday. My doctor called to tell me that the results from my biopsy showed that I had breast cancer. Hearing those words "You have breast cancer" cut me to the core of my soul. My personal life was already in despair. It had been 4 months since I had walked away from a 15-year unhealthy marriage, and surely, I didn't need this bad news. I was not in a good place emotionally, mentally or spiritually. Where did this thing called breast cancer come from? No one in my family had it, so how did I get it? I have 3 sons; how do I tell them that their mother has breast cancer? How do I tell my family this awful news? Was I going to die from it? The Bible says that *"this sickness is not unto death,"* so I had to find an inner strength that I was going to beat cancer. Battling breast cancer and going through a divorce at the same time, was mentally, physically, and emotionally grueling. As the side effects from the radiation took over my body; climbing the stairs, finding the strength to feed myself, and getting in and out of bed became more difficult. My life felt so surreal. Why did this life-threatening disease show up on my doorstep when I was already at the lowest point in my life? How do I cope with the fact that due to no fault of my own, my body has betrayed me? There were days when I couldn't talk to nobody but God, so I began to cry out to Him like I never had before.

I used to be ashamed of my scars, and ashamed of the darkness on my chest because of the radiation treatments. I used to wonder was I less than a woman because parts of me had been altered? I had some serious self-esteem issues to conquer due to this illness. Throughout this journey, I learned that there is something beautiful about using my scars, my mistakes, my struggles, and my flaws to help other people. My external scars do not define me. Going through my journey with breast cancer became a platform for me to help and inspire other people. People have embraced my transparency. I thought that the only way that God could use me was if I did everything right. God showed me that He could use me despite my flaws. God was molding and shaping me to be used by Him through my breast cancer journey. He was making me into the strong and praying woman that I am today.

The spirit of unforgiveness and rage were rising in my soul, and I had to learn the power of forgiveness through my illness. Some people walked away from me during this traumatic time, and I felt betrayed, hurt, and I wanted revenge, but in Romans 12:19, it says *"Vengeance is mine, I will repay,"* says the Lord, so I have to leave it up to God for He knows all and sees all. In hindsight, I now view my diagnosis as a process where the tare had to be separated from the wheat. In the Bible, David said that it was good that he had been afflicted. Likewise, breast cancer was everything that I needed, but nothing I ever wanted. I needed breast cancer and forgiveness to work hand-in-hand in my life; I couldn't have had one or the other. I learned that everything is not God sent, but it is God used. God had a mission and a purpose for me, and through breast cancer, He was refining, and building character and self-worth in me. God will often use our deepest pains as the launching pad of our greatest calling. I needed to be around people who are prayer warriors, and who had my best interest at heart. I am now in peace and not pieces. I thank God for carrying me when I was unable to carry myself.

Breast cancer showed me that I was existing, and not living. In the blink of an eye, your life can change drastically, and you have to learn how to re-shift your priorities. I was always a people pleaser, and for once in my life, I had to shift the focus to myself. I had to fight for the will to live. When trials and tribulations come up in my life now, I don't falter or give up; I keep pressing forward. I have to remind myself that I not only conquered breast cancer, but I am thriving in life every day. Do I get discouraged sometimes? Yes, I do. There are days when the pain from lymphedema, which is a side effect of breast cancer, is overwhelming, and I have trouble reaching and doing daily activities. The side effects are painful, and they are like a thorn in my side, but it reminds me that God will continue to heal me, because there is a greater work that He has for me to do. I want people to find healing in my wounds, and from my deepest hurts. I want to inspire people to keep fighting and to press forward with whatever storms that they are going through in life.

After my diagnosis, I would go to different parks in my area and sit and watch people and write in my journal. I would laugh at the innocence of the little kids in how they played with each other.

When I share the pains of my journey at churches and conferences, I gain strength when I can encourage women that they too can survive whatever obstacles life throws at them. Since my diagnosis, several family members and close friends have been diagnosed with breast cancer, and we rely on each other for support and encouragement. My mantra now is "Don't sweat the small stuff". I wake up every morning with purpose. I feel like a re-birth has taken place. I am grateful for each new day, I'm grateful for the painful storms that I have gone through, and now I know what living life is about.

My favorite scripture in the Bible is Isaiah 66:9, which says, *"I will not cause pain without allowing something new to be born, says the Lord."* (NCV) The pain of breast cancer, divorce, self-esteem issues, multiple surgeries, and grueling sessions of radiation, were all a part of a birthing process. God gave me beauty for ashes. Breast cancer didn't show up in my life to defeat me; it instilled within me a fighting spirit for life. I am soaring in God's favor and glory. I now know who I am and whose I am. I am free emotionally, mentally and spiritually, and it feels so good. My heart and soul have been awakened. I am free from the bondage of pleasing others, free from brokenness, free from the spirit of unforgiveness, and free from dysfunctional relationships.

Mark Twain has a quote that says, *"The two most important days in your life are the day you are born, and the day you find out why."* On January 19, 2011, I found my "why". Have you found yours?

Meditative Point

Think on some trials that you have gone through in your life, and how you grew from them. We ought to always "Grow through what we go through." Did you use your trials to help others? Have you ever considered the fact, that you are being processed while you are going through the process?

Scripture Reference

Romans 8:28
"And we know that all things work together for good to those who love God, to those who are called according to his purpose."

Chapter Three

The Tears of Hannah

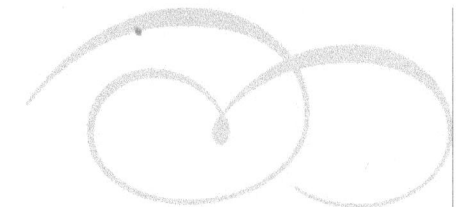

Even as a kid, I've never liked to wait. If you told me that we are going to be somewhere in 15 minutes, I'm looking at the clock counting down the 15 minutes. I'm a person of "order", and I write out my "to do" lists in the morning and plan my day. I plan my calendar in January of events that I want to attend throughout the entire year, and I generally don't leave any wiggle room for adjustments. I practically know what I am going to be doing every hour of my day. I like structure. I like things to be in their proper place. But as the saying goes, "If you want to hear God laugh, tell Him your plans!" I've learned so much about God during the storms over my life these past years, and these storms have changed the essence of who I am.

The story of Hannah in the Bible has so many lessons in it. Hannah was barren, and she desperately wanted a child. In those days, her husband, Elkanah had another wife whose name was Peninnah, and she was able to conceive children. Peninnah has a personality as what we would call today as "petty" or "shady". Peninnah would taunt Hannah of her bareness because Peninnah knew that Elkanah preferred Hannah over her even though Hannah didn't have any children. Every year when Elkanah would offer his sacrifice at the sanctuary, he would give Hannah a double portion because he loved her dearly. Can you imagine year after year, Hannah being taunted by someone because of a flaw that she had no control of? Despite this humiliation, Hannah continued praying to God. One year, Hannah prayed with great "weeping" or as I would say "crying her soul out," and the high priest thought that she was drunk because her mouth was moving, but no words were coming out. Can you imagine praying and travailing in the spirit so hard for something that you longed for, and someone thinks that you are drunk? Can you imagine how Hannah must have felt?

I know all too well of the tears of Hannah. I often relate to my six-year prayer of trying to relocate from Atlanta, GA to Maryland as the "Tears of Hannah." I had requested a job transfer in December 2010, and less than a month later, breast cancer knocked on my door, and my plans had to be readjusted. As I was going through my radiation treatments, I wanted to be near my family in Maryland, so I started requested job transfers again, and I started applying for jobs at other Federal government agencies in Washington, DC, and at Patuxent River, MD. I had even entertained the idea of resigning from the Federal government all together, and I had the attitude of "let's see what happens." Now doesn't that sound a bit crazy? I wanted to come "home" to Maryland so bad, and people would tell me to keep waiting in anticipation. Then I had some Peninnah's that would rise up and say, "Why do you keep praying for a job in Washington, DC year after year when it hasn't happened yet, and have you thought that God doesn't want you to move?" How can I, a person who plans her days, and months out in advance wait when the calendar says differently? This was a test that took me six years to pass, and I must admit that there were some days where I was like "Look here God, I don't want to be made a fool of, but I still want to trust you." There were so many times where I would just sit in my prayer closet and pray to God, "How long must I wait?" There were times when I couldn't even utter the words to pray, and I would cry uncontrollably like Hannah. I knew that I was now living a life unto God, but yet, I felt that God was taking too long to answer my prayer, and the mockeries of the Peninnah's were starting to get to me.

Psalm 39:7 says *"And now, Lord what do I wait for? My hope is in You."* In layman's terms, we could be saying, "Lord, why should I wait this long?" In a way, that sounds very selfish, ungrateful and inconsiderate. When I asked God to send me to Maryland, and when it didn't happen quickly, the human part of me was extremely disappointed. As I dived more into the Word of God and studied the scriptures, I learned to stop grumbling and complaining. The children of Israel wondered in the wilderness for 40 years because of their complaining, and they were only supposed to be on their journey for 11 days. The Peninnah's were sent to distract me, and I had to set my mind that I was going to stay the course because God's word will not return to Him void. I made a vision board, and on it, I put the words "A permanent job in the DMV" and I put a date with this request. I started thanking God daily for my job, even though it hadn't come to pass. I changed my thinking, and I started staying positive. I put a plan in motion that I was leaving Atlanta, GA. I got a storage unit in Maryland, and I started putting my belongings in there. I started writing in a gratitude journal, and I would always write, "God I thank you for sending me home." Even though the calendar year would change, I didn't give up on my dream. I was driving to Maryland at least twice a month by myself, and physically, my body was starting to wear down. I would go on job interviews in Washington, DC, and I would get positive feedback from the interview panel, but yet I wasn't offered a job. There was a "brief" moment when I was thinking, "What more can I do?" I'm doing everything "humanly" possible, and nothing is happening. I even had some employers tell me that I was overly qualified. Really? So, being overly qualified is a bad thing?

In June of 2016, God honored my prayer, and I was offered a job in Washington, DC, and my six-year prayer was not in vain. My years of tears that I laid at the altar were finally over. The Hebrew meaning of the name Hannah is "favor" or "grace". I now understand my tears of Hannah, because God truly bestowed upon me favor and grace with the job that He prepared for me in Washington, DC. To me, this was my Haggai 2:9 (MSG version) *"This temple is going to end up far better than it started out, a glorious beginning but an even more glorious finish."*

Meditative Point

What have you been praying to God for in which you feel that God is taking too long to answer? Do you have the distractions of "Peninnah's" telling you to give up? Hannah did not respond to the attacks of Peninnah's taunting, so the lesson that we can take from this, is that we are to have restraint to not respond to the distractors. Please do not give in to those who are enjoying your setback, because your comeback is going to shut their mouths!

Scripture Reference

Galatians 6:9
"And let us not grow weary while doing good, for in due season we shall reap if we do not lose heart."

Chapter Four

<u>Words Have Power</u>

If the words that you spoke appeared on your skin, would you still be attractive? Negative words and negative emotions are like unwelcomed guests who show up without calling to see if you are home. Just because people show up on our doorsteps, doesn't mean that they have a right to stay. I remember as a child hearing the saying "Sticks and stones will break my bones, but names will never hurt me." I never really thought about the power of words, until verbal abuse started showing up in my life. I've been in relationships in the past where statements were consistently made about my weight, and they were very hurtful, and damaging to my self-esteem. I wasn't always a "curvy" woman, but when you combine years of being on steroid packs for an immune illness, years of breast cancer medication, and toss in being an emotional eater, the weight creeps on, and you one day look up and wonder, "Who am I?" I've been in relationships when men have said to me, "You are going to be fat like certain women in your family." How can someone that says that they love me say this to me, and think that it isn't a hurtful statement?

I once read a quote that says, "If speaking kindly to plants helps them grow, imagine what speaking kindly to humans can do." I pondered on that statement because it is profound. I thought to myself, "Why do people speak such negativity and hurtful statements to other people?" "Why are people so cruel?" In Proverbs 23:7, it states, *"For as a man thinketh in his heart, so is he."* You mean that people can have such hurtful things in their heart, but yet with their mouths they say that they love you? That sounds like a mouthful of lies to me. This has been a tough hurdle that I've dealt with for so many years, and it has really been an emotional rollercoaster. Emotional scars are the deepest, and the most painful scars to heal. I never realized that emotional abuse was a form of domestic abuse. As I look back on my life, my relationships with men have all had the undertone of emotional and verbal abuse. You don't always have to be physically hit to be knocked down. Words have power – whether they are good or bad. I remember women asking me, "Why did I leave my marriage when I wasn't being physically beaten?" Are you kidding me? As women, don't we aspire for more than not being beaten? I didn't get the memo that if you're not being physically abused, and only suffering from verbal or emotional abuse, that at all costs you should stay in an unhealthy relationship.

I was knocked so far down from listening to these negative comments from people that I didn't even know who I was anymore. When people would tell me that I am beautiful, I would look at them like "Are you referring to me?" As years went on, the more that I studied God's Word for myself, I realized that everything that God made was beautiful, and that God didn't make anything ugly. I started praying daily for God to change my thinking, and to heal my heart from the seeds of negativity that had been planted. I started doing daily affirmations such as "I am beautiful!" "I am worthy!" "I am a Queen". The more that I started saying these affirmations, and displaying them on notes on my walls, and mirrors, the more I felt empowered.

Proverbs 18:1 says, *"Death and life are in the power of the tongue, and those who love it will eat its fruit."* We have to be careful who we allow to speak words over us, and also what we speak to ourselves. We have to come to a point in our lives where we can't allow any negativity in our inner space, whether it's from family, friends, co-workers, or significant others. Our lives literally depend on it. The tongue has tremendous power.

Not only do words have power, but we have to be careful with the signage that we wear, and even something as simple as a car tag. I used to have a personalized car tag on a luxury vehicle that said "Lvnglrge", which meant "living large." This was detrimental to my life because the life that I was living and the relationship that I was in was not unto God. We have to be careful of what we proclaim unto God, because we can make things and/or people an idol, and God said in Exodus 20:3 "You shall have no other gods before Me." I eventually lost that vehicle due to a divorce, because it was a leased vehicle I had to turn the vehicle back in. Let me tell you, this humbled me, and it opened up my eyes to what God was trying to tell me. I vowed that when I got another personalized tag that it would be positive. My current car tag says "Hisfav4", which means "His favor." See the difference? I would not be where I am today had it not been for the favor of God. God has brought me to where I am today, and I'm not living an ungodly lifestyle anymore. Let me tell you something, God can humble you to a point that you will see yourself, your life, and people through new eyes.

When men would tell me that I was overweight, and that they wished that I would go back to my former weight when I was in my 20's and early 30's, those statements hurt me deeply. On the covers of magazines, we see thin women, and society tends to paint a picture that a curvier woman is not worthy or that she is extremely unhealthy. I know of some women who are thin, and they are unhealthy, and they take high blood pressure and cholesterol medication. Women can get so caught up in with their weight, and those three digits on the scale. What about her self-worth? What about her inward beauty? What about her soul? If she isn't a size 6, does that mean that she isn't worthy?

One single word from a person can generally make you like or dislike them. If you are around a person who is always complaining or always full of gloom or doom, it can be irritating, and if you are not careful, their grim outlook can rub off on you. You may even wonder; can they have anything positive to say? Are they even thankful for waking up in the morning? I had to let go of some relationships and friendships to go to the next level that God had for me. I couldn't allow any more negative comments or people in my life. It was hard to let these people go but, it has been good for my emotional, mental, and spiritual health. God has placed people in my life who are uplifting, people who are positive, people that can speak life into me, and to my situations. I read somewhere that we are likened to the five people that we hang around. I now see some truth in this, since the people that I now surround myself with are positive and uplifting people. Maybe you need to ask yourself, "Who are the five people that you associate with daily?" After this evaluation, you may come to the conclusion that you need to reevaluate your circle and make some immediate changes. God spoke some powerful words in the Bible, such as "I have come that they may have life, and that they may have it more abundantly." If God whom we serve is speaking life over us, and then saying that we may have it abundantly, how dare we allow a person to speak differently, or to curse what God has said! If we are free in Christ, we need to speak it, walk it, talk it and most of all, live it. When the enemy comes in and tries to place doubt in your life, you need to remind that devil of who you are, and whose you are. We are NOT punks ~ we don't run from the enemy; the enemy runs from us!

Meditative Point

What are you speaking over your own life? Take an inventory on who is in your circle, and make sure that they are "life-speaking" people. Write positive affirmations to yourself and put them on your wall, bathroom mirror, or cubicle, and recite them to yourself every day. Recite every day, "I will slay the Goliaths that may come my way, I am victorious!"

Scripture Reference

Ephesians 4:29
"Let no corrupt word proceed out of your mouth, but what is good for necessary edification, that it may impart grace to the hearers."

Chapter Five

When God Interrupts Your Life

Have you ever been watching your favorite show on TV, and then a message comes on the screen that says, "We interrupt this program to bring you this important message", and then some sort of emergency broadcast displays? Isn't this irritating when you are enjoying your favorite show on TV? You are thinking "Really, why now?" My show on TV was so good, and this message is messing up my vibe!

A financial storm, a marital storm, an unemployment storm, or a health storm, can interrupt your regularly scheduled program called "Life." Here you are minding your own business, and a storm comes and knocks you off your feet. Some storms come with no warning, and no time to prepare for them.

I think about the disciples that were with Jesus on the boat, and there came about a great storm on the Sea of Galilee, and Jesus went to sleep. The waves were hitting fiercely against the boat, and the boat was rocking back and forth, and the boat was filling with water. I can only imagine how frightened those on the boat were, and yet, here is Jesus asleep, and not just in a light sleep, but Jesus was in a deep sleep. I am inclined to think that in our thought process today, we would be thinking, how in the world could Jesus be sound asleep with all of the noise of the outside world going on? Could this be that even those of us who proclaim that we are grounded in God, can be shaken when a storm arises, or when God interrupts our daily lives to mold us and shape us unto Him? When we feel that our life has been interrupted and God seems "quiet" or "asleep", do we think that God has forgotten about us? Do we think and say to God, "Where are you?" When you gave God your "yes", did you think that your life would be smooth sailing? In John 16:33, it says "These things I have spoken unto you, that in Me you have peace. In the world you will have tribulation; but be of good cheer, I have overcome the world."

I can remember on multiple times where I felt that God interrupted my life. Now doesn't that sound crazy to say the words "my life", when my life really belongs to God?" I've had so many storms in my life, health, financial, marital, mental, spiritual, and emotional, and some of these storms occurred at the same time. I would wonder "Why is this happening all at once, and God where are you?" Sometimes it seemed to me that God was silent, or as Jesus was on the ship "sound asleep". I had planned out certain things in my life of places that I wanted to go, and things that I wanted to do, and here comes some sort of storm, or in reality God was interrupting my life to get my attention. Sometimes we can go out of the will of God, and of course God knows the plans that He has for us, and I feel that God is like "Oh no, son or daughter, I can't let you go too far into sin, I have work for you to do for the Kingdom, so I need you to come to your senses and come back to Me." Have you ever been in this situation? I know that I have. I remember being a people pleaser to a point that I started operating outside of the will of God to please a man. There was nothing that I wouldn't do in this relationship to please him, not matter how immoral it was. I remember at one point, I thought of the prodigal son, and how my life was starting to reflect it. I was in the pig pen of an unhealthy relationship, a pig pen of sexual immorality, a pig pen of spiritual abuse, and I wanted God to save me from the humiliation I was experiencing. I would pray, but I honestly felt that God was not listening to me. I thought that I had gone too far where God couldn't hear me. In Deuteronomy 31:8 it says, "And the Lord, He is the One who goes before you. He will be with you, He will never leave you nor forsake you; do not be dismayed." I am thankful to God for not allowing the devil to consume me even when I had placed myself in situations to be consumed.

The people that I was around for so many years showed me that you can have a title in a church if you want, but what really matters is that you have a Godly relationship. God in their bio does not mean God in their life. Satan starts with luring you in subtly, and before you know it, you can be caught up in a world of sin and you can't figure out how you got there. Date nights turned into weekly visits to the strip club, card parties at my residence displayed the fornication and adultery that was occurring. There was even a lifestyle of sharing partners, but yet, these were people who had titles in the church that I was around. I was so conflicted because this was all "new" to me. My prior upbringing in church NEVER consisted of all of this sin. People refer to Atlanta as Sodom and Gomorrah and soon, I began to understand why. We (there were Pastors included), were living a life of sin throughout the week and on Sunday, the Pastor is preaching his heart out, and people are shouting and dancing in the church. After many years of feeling like a zombie in this lifestyle, I "came to myself" such as the Prodigal Son and I repented and vowed to NEVER, EVER go back to that lifestyle of sin. Then I gave God my "Yes". Now, you do know that when you give God your "yes", your life will never be the same. God will interrupt the mess you are in to get you back to Him. Now I know that it wasn't that God was silent, He was waiting on me to come to my senses. Have your parents ever said to you before when you've gotten in trouble, "Don't make me have to knock some sense into you?" Could the interruptions in our lives be that God is trying to "knock some sense into us?" I wonder does God say to himself, "Why does she/he have to go through all of that, when if he/she had listened to Me the first time, they wouldn't have to go through this?" I remember saying the very same thing with my children. I would tell them things to do, things that I expected of them, pick your clothes up off of the floor, keep your bathroom clean, keep your room clean, and it seemed like the more I said it, the more my requests would be ignored. Then I would say "I'm tired of talking to you over and over about the same thing, and I am going to take some things away from you, like the cell phone, X-box etc." Don't you think that God gets fed up with telling us things over and over again? Don't you think that God wants us to learn the lesson the first time? Why must we have to go through a life-threatening illness, a divorce (when God didn't send you that person), or even financial hardships (living beyond our means), when God has told us that we are to live Holy and righteous before Him. I know that some of us can be stubborn, but don't let your stubbornness cost you to delay what God has destined for you to have or to be.

I don't want you to think that we won't ever experience storms in life, because we will, for that is a part of our walk with Christ. We need to hold fast and stand boldly and be confident in the fact that whatever we may experience in life - we are going to stand firm on the promises of God. Do not live a life of gloom and doom. Do not allow past emotions of bitterness, resentment, anger, hurt or pain to keep you bound. Christ said, "Whom the Son sets free is free indeed." Now I've learned to take everything to God in prayer, whether it is a financial decision, or people that try to enter into my life. I don't want God to have to interrupt my life again to the point that the storm feels like I'm drowning in it. I know that trials and tests will come, but if we learn the lessons the first time, we won't have to keep repeating the same lessons over and over again.

Meditative Point

Are there areas in your life that need to be changed? Look at the tests and trials that you have gone through and/or going through and if they are the same tests, why? Don't let your interruption be something life-threatening for God to get your attention. I want you to think about this quote that I once read: "Sin ~ it takes you where you don't want to go, it keeps you longer than you want to stay, and it costs you more than you want to pay."

Scripture Reference

Romans 6:23
"For the wages of sin is death, but the gift of God is eternal life in Christ Jesus our Lord."

Chapter Six

Spiritual Health

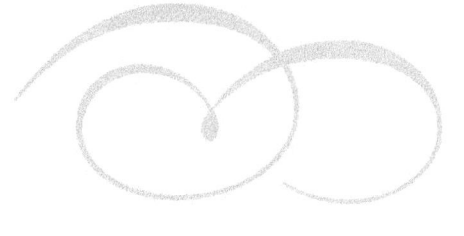

In the natural world, we are required to get yearly physicals. The doctor does a thorough exam, and if the doctor finds something abnormal during the exam, the doctor will give you recommendations on what to do to correct those abnormalities. We typically follow the recommendations and go back to the doctor's office to get an updated report. Have you ever thought about your spiritual health, and if it needs a check-up? God is not only concerned about our physical health, but He is also concerned about our mind, body and soul. The Bible says in 3rd John 2:2, "Beloved, I pray that you may prosper in all things and be in health, just as your soul prospers." It says "ALL" things, not some, not a few, but ALL. Do you choose to be around people who are life giving, or do you choose to be around people who are life taking? What you think about, and who you commune with influences your spiritual health. Do you have people around you that drain you mentally and emotionally, or do you have people in your life that stimulate your mind and provide nourishment to our soul? The people that we choose to have in our lives will directly affect our total being.

I've had to evaluate who I had in my life, and whether they were good for my spiritual health. The Bible tells us in 1st Corinthians 11:28 (in part), "But let a man examine himself." I believe that the beginning part of this scripture, is telling us to look inward, and do some self-checks, and also some soul and heart checks. This scripture is used before communion service as it should be, and in essence, shouldn't our spiritual health be in its best shape as we are about to partake in a ceremony as sacred as The Lord's Supper? I believe that it should be. How can we come before God with inner spiritual abnormalities, and expect a good report? We don't get those same results from our natural doctor, so why should we expect to come before God with so many blemishes, and not expect there to be some need for corrections?

There are times in our spiritual lives where we will experience what could be deemed as an adverse spiritual report. What exactly does this mean? If you have a food allergy and you eat something that you are allergic to, you will have what is called an adverse reaction. Your body is rejecting something that it has deemed foreign, and you will get sick. The same will happen in our spiritual lives. We fall back into sin, and we rekindle toxic relationships out of loneliness, and the Holy Spirit starts rejecting this because sin has become foreign to the spiritual man, and you have an adverse reaction. Sin can make you feel guilty, and you can become disconnected from God. This is why it is so important to our spiritual health that we feed it correctly just as we are supposed to feed our natural body in the same manner.

Meditative Point

Pray and ask God to do a spiritual check-up in your life. Ask God to remove anything and anyone that is not lining up with His word. When God gives you the answer, take heed, and don't procrastinate, it is extremely important to be healthy in your body, your mind, and in your spirit.

Scripture Reference

Jeremiah 33:6
"Behold, I will bring it health and healing; I will heal them and reveal to them the abundance of peace and truth."

Chapter Seven

The Box

As a PK (Pastor's Kid), people will always try to put you in a box. I am pretty sure that many PK's will agree with me. You are automatically labeled, and some of those labels may not be necessarily true, but they exist anyway. Coming up in the Apostolic doctrine, I felt that some of the mandatory "don'ts" didn't make sense to me. It was hard for me as a teenager not being able to wear pants, and the boys would make fun of me and call me "church girl" all of the time. I promised myself that when I got "grown" that I was not going to wear dresses, and that my closet would be full of pants (rebellion). It's kind of funny because to this day, I have several closets, and they are full of dresses, and I may have no more than 10 pairs of pants.

My natural hair is a sandy brown color, and it is naturally curly. When I was in middle school, some people would make fun of my hair and say "She thinks that she's cute because she has good hair." What exactly is good hair? The other girls were getting what was called "relaxers", and I wanted to get one also, so that I wouldn't be teased anymore. My parents agreed to my request of getting a relaxer, and I went to the local beauty salon to get my hair done because I wanted to fit in with the girls at school. I was allowing other people to put me in a box, which later transcended into my adult hood.

As I embarked into relationships with men, I allowed them to put me in a box to a point where the relationships became controlling and toxic. One man would only "allow" me to wear my hair a certain way, and that was straight. He wouldn't "allow" me to wear colored polish on my fingernails, and I could only wear red polish on my toes, and he preferred hair on my legs, so I couldn't shave them. All of these were things that I hated, and before I met him, I did the exact opposite. Why did I allow him to put me in a box? How could this be called love when you lose your identity? I felt like a captive in this relationship, and once that relationship ended; I felt that I had escaped Alcatraz.

Meditative Point

If you have allowed people to put you into a box, break free TODAY! You have opinions, you have a voice, and you have a mind. Get out of bondage and live a life full of freedom that God intended you to live.

Scripture Reference

John 8:36
"Therefore, if the Son makes you free, you shall be free indeed."

Chapter Eight

Is My "Yes" Negotiable?

Have you ever said "God, I will serve you, but just let me finish this sin or let me get my life together first?" I remember in middle school, boys would send a girl a letter saying, "Do you like me, check the box, yes, no or maybe." Isn't that what we do to God sometimes? We want to serve God, but we don't want to lose the friends, or we may feel that the person that we are in a relationship with will leave.

There is a song by a group called Shekinah Glory called "Yes" and in the extended version of the song some of the lyrics are "After we've given our all, God still wants a Yes. Some of us He called a long time ago, and yet we're doing what we want to do, we're picking and choosing our Yes. But God is saying, all I want is Yes. Be careful, because Yes might cost you everything." How many of you have been in this predicament? Let me be transparent and say that I have, multiple times. I always knew that there was a calling on my life as a teenager, but I wanted to fit in. I didn't like it when the kids would tease me and say, "Here comes the church girl," or the boys would say, "She can't go anywhere, but to church." Those words hurt my feelings, and I was torn. I loved God, but I also wanted to "fit in". Even in relationships, I compromised my "Yes" for God. I would get into relationships that

I knew that God didn't ordain because I thought that if I prayed hard enough, that the person would change. God isn't obligated to bless a relationship that was not ordained by Him.

God says in Revelation 3:16 (NLT), "but since you are like lukewarm water, neither hot nor cold, I will spit you out of my mouth!" That scripture steps on a bunch of toes, but don't we say something similar to that in our friendships and/or relationships? We tell people, either you are in my corner or not, I can't have people riding the fence. So, if we expect people to be fully committed to us, why can't we be fully committed to God without negotiating? What gives us the right to say, "God if you get me out of this situation, I will serve you?" What if God doesn't deliver you out whatever you are in, will you still give him your Yes?

Meditative Point

Examine where you are in your spiritual life and honestly ask yourself, "Have I given God a full Yes?" If you haven't, why not? How long do you think that God is going to allow you to sit on the fence? Have you ever considered that you are unique, and your calling and/or your gift is what someone needs?

Scripture Reference

Mark 8:34
"Whoever desires to come after Me, let him deny himself, and take up his cross, and follow me."

Chapter Nine

The Tsunami Called Grief

One of the definitions of a Tsunami is: an arrival of something in overwhelming quantities or amounts.

We have all dealt with grief at some point in our lives, whether it's a parent, cousin, pet, or a close friend. Here I was excited about the last month of December 2018 and looking forward to ending the year on a high note. December has always been my favorite month of the year (next to my birthday in March), because I love the magic of Christmas. I've always been fascinated by the Christmas lights, all of the holiday decorations, and spending time with my family. I never imagined in a million years, that I was about to be hit with a tsunami that has forever changed me. Usually when a storm such as a tsunami or a hurricane comes, the meteorologist will warn the residents instructing them when it is the approximate time for them to take cover, and board up their homes, or in some severe cases, when to leave their homes or cities. A warning is sent forth and most of the time, residents adhere to the warning, and prepare for what is to come.

On December 3, 2018, I received a call that my youngest son, Darryl, had been shot and killed in Atlanta, GA. To me, this storm was a tsunami. It has been the biggest storm that I have faced in my entire life. I didn't get a warning that this storm was about to happen, there weren't any signs from God, nor did a prophet sent from God give me a "word" for me to prepare. I vividly remember when I heard the words on the phone that "my son is dead", I started screaming to the top of my lungs, and fell to the floor. My parents and I left Maryland hours later to drive to Atlanta, GA which is a 10-hour road trip, I remember crying the entire time. I've cried before when relatives or friends have died, but these tears, and the overwhelming sense of grief was unbearable. I hadn't communicated with my ex-husband since 2010, and now we are faced with a parent's worst nightmare. How do we cope with the death of our son? How do we cope with facing each other after having gone through a painful divorce? So many emotions were running through my mind, as well as questions of how did this happen, and who did this? As the days of dealing with funeral arrangements passed, my son's death brought about forgiveness between me and my ex-husband. It was like a weight was lifted between us. Why did it take the tragedy of our son for us to communicate again? We didn't have a manual on how to grieve, so we have relied on each other for the grieving process. Sometimes, I would get angry at some of the texts, and comments that people would say such as "How was your son's service, I'm sure that it was great?" or "You know that your son had to be sacrificed." or the one that really made me angry was "You've dealt with breast cancer, so you will get through this too." I wish that there was some type of etiquette for people to follow when someone is grieving because these types of comments made my grief process harder, and I could feel anger rising up in me. I've had people say to me that they know what I am going through; yet, they haven't had a child to die, so they can't possibly know the extreme amount of grief that I felt.

I remember saying to my ex-husband that we can't ask God "Why did this happen", but instead we have to ask, "What can we learn from this?" Some of the things that I have learned from this storm of grief is sincere forgiveness. I'm not talking about the type of forgiveness where a person gives a halfway apology, but I've experienced a public form of forgiveness, a raw type of forgiveness, and a spiritual release type of forgiveness. This grieving process has been multi-layered such as a natural tsunami. I never saw this type of storm coming, I wasn't warned, and I didn't have time to prepare for it. A tsunami comes to bring severe destruction, and in a way the tsunami of grief, almost destroyed me as a person. My faith was shaken, and most days it felt like I was walking through a thick fog, and I felt like I didn't have control over my emotions.

What I've learned is that a person must grieve in their own way, and that there isn't a "right or a wrong" way to grieve. I am a strong woman, but the pain of losing my son can't be described, but I know that as time goes on, the grief will lessen. The devil was trying to make me feel as if God didn't love me because of this tragedy, and that this happened to my family because I gave God my full "Yes." The devil is nothing but a liar. I had to serve notice to the devil that this tsunami of grief was not going to be the demise of me because "Strong walls shake, but they don't collapse!"

I asked God to send some people my way whom have experienced losing a child to help me with the grieving process, and God honored my prayer. These women have been my anchor and we can share our pain, and we understand clearly what each of us are feeling.

Even in your darkest hour, God will send help. This grieving process has been hard, it's been long, and I cry every day. This tsunami has birthed reconciliation of families, it has made parents discuss with their children the importance of being cautious of who their friends are, it has started conversations within the church, that there has to be real conversations of the tactics that the devil will use. If the devil can't get to a person directly, he will attack your bloodline. We can't just quote scriptures, and not know the culture of this wicked world, we must watch as well as pray.

Meditative points

Dealing with the grief of a sudden death of a child can be devasting. Do not allow anyone to tell you how you should grieve. Do not keep your feelings inside, you may feel that you don't have anyone to talk too, but you should talk to God. He will heal your heart, in time.

Scripture

Psalm 34:18 (NCV)
"The Lord is close to the brokenhearted, and he saves those whose spirits have been crushed."

Poems Inspired by The Storm

I Am A Woman

I am a woman that has endured multiple breast surgeries, and my battle scars are a daily reminder, that I've overcome a life-threatening illness and won.

I am a woman that has had to come face to face with my own mortality, and it made me realize that I was just existing and not living.

I am a woman who is similar to Job, I lost worldly possessions, some family and some friends, but also like Job, I believe that God will give me double for my trouble. I believe in Joel 2:25 that God will repay unto me the years that the locusts have eaten.

I am a woman that kept propping herself up on people, and being so dependent on them, that God took away my crutches and forced me to trust in Him.

I am a woman who is clothed in strength and dignity, and I laugh without fear of the future. I am a virtuous woman, a godly woman, a conquer, and a fighter.

I am a woman that is no longer a people pleaser, and I know that every person is not going to understand my journey, and my purpose. They have a right to their opinions, and negative comments, and I have every right to ignore it.

I am a woman who had to learn that there is power in forgiveness. Forgiveness started with me forgiving myself which allowed me to live in the freedom that God has destined for me.

Finally, I am a woman that has finally found calmness within herself, because I'm in peace ~ not in pieces.

Dear Butterfly

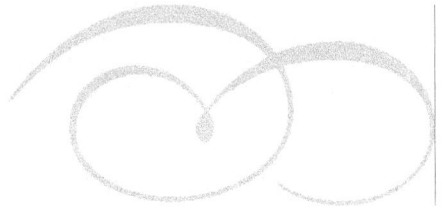

You were born to fly. You were born to be a free spirit. Most of your life, you were like a caterpillar, just creeping along, existing but never living. Then your metamorphosis came, and not only changed you on the inside, but it gave you a glow on the outside. The struggles that you went through gave you beauty for ashes. Your inner beauty is captivating. Your struggles gave you wings, your struggles made you free, your storms made you fly. Never stop flying!

<u>New Beginnings</u>

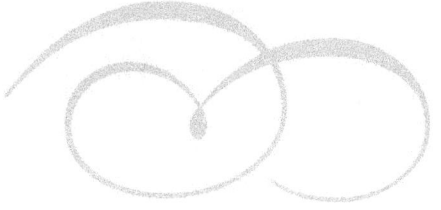

Transitioning can be hard, scary, exciting, rewarding, and awkward. How do you go forth into the unknown? Do you think of failure? Do you think of being a conqueror? If you've had heartbreak, how soon do you let your guard down to love again? New beginnings can give you a feeling of freedom. Only your inner soul knows your thoughts. It can be a feeling of a weight being lifted off of your shoulders, and you never knew how heavy the weight was until it's gone. Today, why don't you look forward and move ahead? What's stopping you? Could it be your self-doubt? Could it be your inner fears? Toss those insecurities aside and launch out into the deep. Who knows, everything you've dreamed of and more is waiting for you.

God Had A Plan

I know where my life is headed from here and even in my holding patterns, I have maintained a peaceful feeling. All the sacrifices have been worth it. I've seen forgiveness take place in the most unconventional places.

There's something so beautiful about using your scars, your mistakes, your heartaches, your pain, your struggles, and your insecurities to help others.

I never thought that the pain would be worth it. The cost of the oil in my Alabaster Box has been great, and I wouldn't change any part of my journey, because God had a plan.

<u>A House vs. A Home</u>

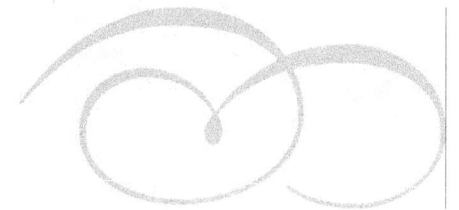

It's not the material things that make a house a home. It's the family that you have inside of it. To me, a home is supposed to be a place of peace, a safe haven, a place of love, forgiveness, laughter, joy, and acceptance. I don't recall experiencing that as an adult in my relationships with men. I've had numerous houses, but emotionally, I was homeless.

The Darkest Moments Defined My Life

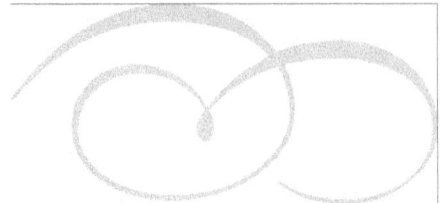

How did the darkest moments define my life? They taught me who was there for me. They taught me that I have to rely solely on God. They increased my faith and Bible studying. My spirit became quiet, and I was able to hear the voice of God clearly. My spiritual vision and discernment got clearer. I took time out for me and I learned who I was. Family ties grew stronger and ultimately, forgiveness became easier.

Even good people go through dark moments. Sickness will cause you to know that God is a healer. I've known God as a comforter when I'm lying in the bed in the wee hours of the night with tears running down my face. I would often wonder why is God so quiet when you are going through a test? We know that He is a teacher and every teacher does all of their talking and all of their teaching before the test. What I found out is that, if you are a good student, what the teacher put in you before the test, will be what comes out of you in the middle of the test. The answer is within you.

My Journey

I didn't choose my breast cancer journey, in fact, it chose me. I didn't ask for breast cancer to bring me back to God, yet, I'm eternally grateful that it did. I didn't ask for breast cancer to teach me how to forgive, yet, I desperately needed it to do so. My journey with breast cancer will always be a big part of my life, and it's impossible for me to forget that it happened. I would not be doing all that God has called me to do, had breast cancer not given me the "wake-up" call.

Doctors say to embrace "your new normal." To be honest, nothing for me has been normal since my diagnosis. I never got a chance to grieve "me", as so many women decide to do so when they are diagnosed with cancer. Instead, I chose to hit the ground running with trying to be the super hero to other women, and to inspire them on their own journeys.

Now that I've conquered breast cancer, I'm grateful for it helping me to discover the fighting spirit within. It is amazing how those four words, "You have breast cancer," can change your life. As I continue to celebrate LIFE, I can now say that "I had breast cancer, but breast cancer never had me!"

The Invisible Chain

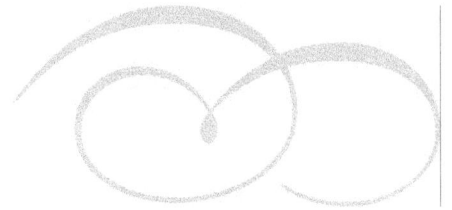

How did these invisible chains become a part of my daily attire? How did I get to this place of church hurt? I never was in a play before, yet I have a starting role in a position that I didn't audition for. What goes on behind closed doors is supposed to stay there is what we are told. As wives of men in the church who hold positions, we are NOT supposed to say anything about the abuse: whether it's physical, mental, sexual, or emotional. We come to church year after year, and sit in our perfectly assigned pew, wear our perfect suit, wear our perfect hat, and wear the prefect shade of lipstick ~~not too bright of a color of lipstick because the "worldly women" wear bright colors. If we voice our opinions on anything, our husbands know how to tightly pull the invisible chains around our necks to put us back in line. We are not supposed to say anything about the women who run up to our husbands after church as they wait in line for the "church hug" that seems to last a little longer than it should. We see ~ but we don't see. We are supposed to act like a classy lady upon entering the sanctuary, but yet our husband has just cussed us out in the car on the way to church. Hold your head up sister, shake it off, you have a starring role that you must adhere too. Hide your emotions, play your part, because if you don't, there are many women in the church who want to take your role from you.

What are these invisible chains? They are chains of religion. They are invisible chains of undocumented doctrine and rules. They are invisible chains of control, and invisible chains of generational church abuse. So many women in the church have these chains around their necks. We are screaming at the top of our lungs for someone to save us – but no one will answer our screams. We have to come into the sanctuary with our heads held high, we have to sit through the sermons, and we don't hear what the pastor is preaching because our minds are somewhere else. Who will come to our rescue? The Bible says that if you're sick, call for the Elders of the church. This abuse is a sickness and it's at the hands of those who are supposed to pray for us, so who will save us?

One day, I decided to be bold and speak up about an incident to my husband, and when I did, the invisible chains were pulled tightly, and I was called every name BUT a child of God. Help me, my inner spirit cried ~~ I can't breathe. It feels like I'm having an asthma attack. I was reminded that women are not to speak in the church; women are to do whatever their husbands say. We are told that it's our fault as to why we are being abused physically, mentally, sexually, and verbally. We are told that we aren't praying enough for our husbands because surely, it's something that "WE" are doing for this to have happened.

Years and years had passed, and one day, I got sick and tired of being sick and tired, and I started praying to God. God please provide me with a way of escape. Lord, please forgive me for making religion an idol god; please forgive me for putting "man" on a pedestal. Father God, if you provide a way out for me, I will NOT look back like the wife of Lot. I will help other women escape these invisible prison cells of religion. I will help other women get these invisible chains from around their necks. I feel myself gaining strength, I am hearing the voice of God clearly, and I see God's hand reaching down to me to run to Him. I start taking baby steps…one step…two steps…three steps ~ then I find myself running towards God. I'm running for my life ~ literally! I feel the invisible chains falling. I inhale…exhale…. inhale…exhale --- my God, I'm breathing on my own again. The strongholds of abuse have been released. I run into the arms of God and HE provides a safety net for me. He lets me know who I am, and whose I am.

The invisible chains are running rampant in the church, but the church doesn't want to talk about it. It's swept under the rug. Where are the women that want the invisible chains removed? Where are the women that want to kick down the doors of the cliché "What goes on behind closed doors should stay behind closed doors?" Where are the women that are sick and tired of being sick and tired? Where are the women who are tired of suffering from a church encounter, but they aspire to have a God encounter? I am thankful for the women that have taken a stand to run to God, and their invisible chains have been released. Yes, I pray for the women who decided to stay invisibly chained. Wake up my sister, whom the Son sets free, is free indeed.

Aaaaahhhhhhh, it feels so good to breathe fresh air. It feels so good to have been FOREVER released from my invisible chains!

30 Day Journal

30 Day Journal

Day 1

30 Day Journal

Day 2

30 Day Journal

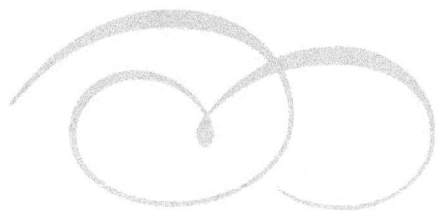

Day 3

30 Day Journal

Day 4

30 Day Journal

Day 5

30 Day Journal

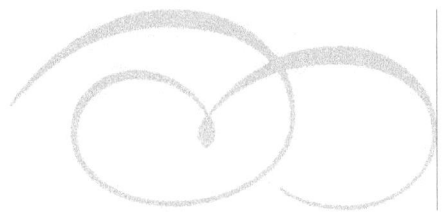

Day 6

30 Day Journal

Day 7

30 Day Journal

Day 8

30 Day Journal

Day 9

30 Day Journal

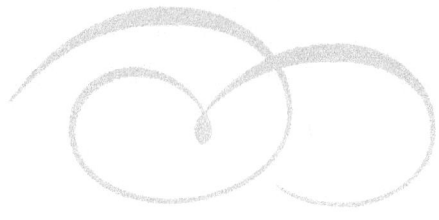

Day 10

30 Day Journal

Day 11

30 Day Journal

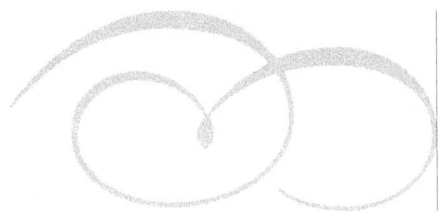

Day 12

30 Day Journal

Day 13

30 Day Journal

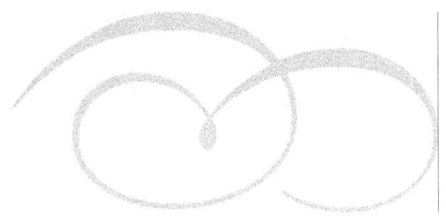

Day 14

30 Day Journal

Day 15

30 Day Journal

Day 16

30 Day Journal

Day 17

30 Day Journal

Day 18

30 Day Journal

Day 19

30 Day Journal

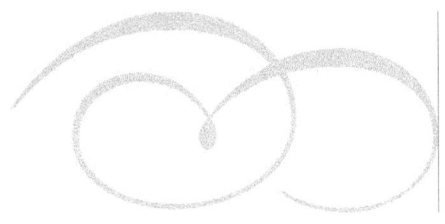

Day 20

30 Day Journal

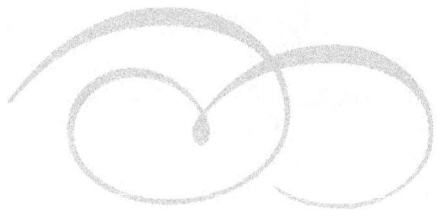

Day 21

30 Day Journal

Day 22

30 Day Journal

Day 23

30 Day Journal

Day 24

30 Day Journal

Day 25

30 Day Journal

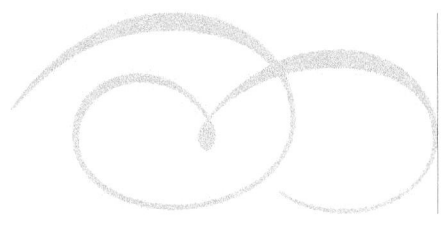

Day 26

30 Day Journal

Day 27

30 Day Journal

Day 28

30 Day Journal

Day 29

30 Day Journal

Day 30

About the Author

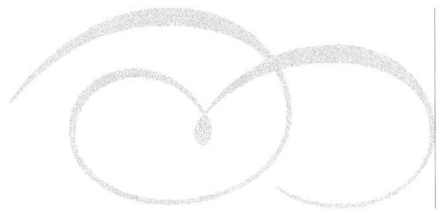

Wanda S. Briscoe is a native of St. Mary's County, Maryland. Wanda moved to Atlanta, Georgia in 1991, and resided there until 2016. Wanda prayed for many years that God would send her back to Maryland, and in the summer of 2016, God honored her request.

Wanda was diagnosed with breast cancer in 2011, and she was the first person in her family to be diagnosed with this life-threatening disease. Wanda didn't see breast cancer as a death sentence, but in turn, she saw it as a life sentence, it was a reason to live. Wanda started educating others about the disease, and wrote her first book in 2012, called "The Fight Within", which is about her breast cancer journey. Wanda has become a mentor to many women as they have embarked on their own breast cancer journeys.

Wanda is active in the breast cancer sisterhood group in St. Mary's County, MD, called "Pink ~ Bold ~ and Beautiful. Wanda has a servant's heart, and she is always helping others, not only in their breast cancer journey, but to navigate through the trials of life. Those that know her know that they can contact her anytime for prayer, or just to talk, and that they will leave the conversation feeling inspired.

Wanda is a sought-after inspirational speaker, and she loves uplifting others by sharing her stories of triumph. Wanda has received accolades from her first book "The Fight Within" from the former First Lady Michelle Obama, and also from Bishop T.D. Jakes of "The Potters House" in Dallas, Texas. Wanda's book "The Fight Within" is also in several cancer center libraries for their patient reading. In 2014, Wanda co-authored an inspirational book called "The Art of Activation" with 23 other authors from around the country.

In 2018, Wanda launched her first business called Mariposa Enterprises, LLC. Mariposa Enterprises' mission is to provide support to the whole person (mind, body, spirit) by providing them with educational information, community connections, and spiritual support as they are going through the entire cancer journey (diagnosis, treatment, and recovery).

Wanda is the proud mother of two adult sons, (a third son is now deceased). Wanda currently resides in St. Mary's County, Maryland.

My closing thoughts:

There is a beautiful song called "Blessings" by Laura Story, and I want to leave these powerful words with you to reinforce the beauty of a storm: "What if trials of this life, the rain, the storms, the hardest nights, are your mercies in disguise." In essence, The Storm Has A Ministry Too!!

You can contact Wanda S. Briscoe using the mediums below:
Email: mariposaenterpriseswsb@gmail.com
Website: www.wandabriscoe.org

Other Books By the Author

The Fight Within

In her first book published in 2012, Wanda S. Briscoe beckons you to travel a journey with her as she shares her personal story of dealing with the emotional, mental, and spiritual road with battling breast cancer. The pain has brought her to her purpose and it allowed her to step into her destiny. You too can thrive through any adversity that you may encounter, because there is a Fight Within in all of us.

<u>The Art of Activation</u>
<u>24 Laws to Win, To Thrive, To Prosper, To Rise</u>

Wanda was one of twenty four contributing authors of The Art of Activation. Wanda shares her chapter entitled, "Using the Power of Forgiveness." In this chapter, Wanda talks about her challenges, trials, and tragedies, as well as her victories. Wanda states, "God gave me beauty for ashes, forgiveness gave me strength, victory and healing. I am not my past; I am that which has emerged from the fire. I am a woman that has finally found calmness within herself through forgiveness, because I now walk in peace ~ and not pieces!"

About the Publisher

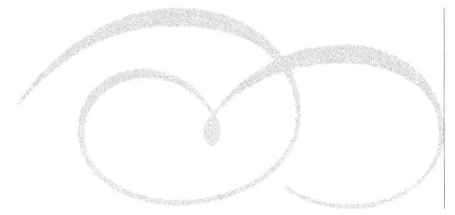

At **Vision to Fruition Publishing House**, we are dedicated to helping others bring their personal, business, ministry & nonprofit visions to fruition.

Whether it's as grand as a book you want to write, a business you want to start, a conference or event you want to host, a ministry you want to launch or an organization you want to start; or as small as needing a computer repair, logo design or web design; **Vision to Fruition Publishing House** will help you walk through the process and set you up for success! At **Vision to Fruition** we don't have clients, we have **Visionaries**. We provide solutions to equip others to pursue their visions & dreams with reckless abandon.

We have published more than twenty-three authors, several of which were #1 Amazon Bestsellers. We would love for you to join our family of Visionaries as well!!!

Learn more here: www.vision-fruition.com

www.ingramcontent.com/pod-product-compliance
Lightning Source LLC
Chambersburg PA
CBHW070303100426
42743CB00011B/2326